I0454694

Editor-in-Chief and Founder:
Lyndon H. LaRouche, Jr.
Editorial Board: *Lyndon H. LaRouche, Jr. , Helga Zepp-LaRouche, Robert Ingraham, Tony Papert, Gerald Rose, Dennis Small, Jeffrey Steinberg, William Wertz*
Co-Editors: *Robert Ingraham, Tony Papert*
Managing Editor: *Nancy Spannaus*
Technology: *Marsha Freeman*
Books: *Katherine Notley*
Ebooks: *Richard Burden*
Graphics: *Alan Yue*
Photos: *Stuart Lewis*
Circulation Manager: *Stanley Ezrol*

INTELLIGENCE DIRECTORS
Counterintelligence: *Jeffrey Steinberg, Michele Steinberg*
Economics: *John Hoefle, Marcia Merry Baker, Paul Gallagher*
History: *Anton Chaitkin*
Ibero-America: *Dennis Small*
Russia and Eastern Europe: *Rachel Douglas*
United States: *Debra Freeman*

INTERNATIONAL BUREAUS
Bogotá: *Miriam Redondo*
Berlin: *Rainer Apel*
Copenhagen: *Tom Gillesberg*
Houston: *Harley Schlanger*
Lima: *Sara Madueño*
Melbourne: *Robert Barwick*
Mexico City: *Gerardo Castilleja Chávez*
New Delhi: *Ramtanu Maitra*
Paris: *Christine Bierre*
Stockholm: *Ulf Sandmark*
United Nations, N.Y.C.: *Leni Rubinstein*
Washington, D.C.: *William Jones*
Wiesbaden: *Göran Haglund*

ON THE WEB
e-mail: eirns@larouchepub.com
www.larouchepub.com
www.executiveintelligencereview.com
www.larouchepub.com/eiw
Webmaster: *John Sigerson*
Assistant Webmaster: *George Hollis*
Editor, Arabic-language edition: *Hussein Askary*

EIR (ISSN 0273-6314) *is published weekly (50 issues), by EIR News Service, Inc., P.O. Box 17390, Washington, D.C. 20041-0390. (703) 777-9451 ext. 415*

European Headquarters: E.I.R. GmbH, Postfach Bahnstrasse 9a, D-65205, Wiesbaden, Germany
Tel: 49-611-73650
Homepage: http://www.eirna.com
e-mail: eirna@eirna.com
Director: Georg Neudecker

Montreal, Canada: 514-461-1557

Denmark: EIR - Danmark, Sankt Knuds Vej 11, basement left, DK-1903 Frederiksberg, Denmark. Tel.: +45 35 43 60 40, Fax: +45 35 43 87 57. e-mail: eirdk@hotmail.com.

Mexico City: EIR, Sor Juana Inés de la Cruz 242-2 Col. Agricultura C.P. 11360 Delegación M. Hidalgo, México D.F. Tel. (5525) 5318-2301 eirmexico@gmail.com

Canada Post Publication Sales Agreement #40683579

Postmaster: Send all address changes to *EIR*, P.O. Box 17390, Washington, D.C. 20041-0390.

Signed articles in *EIR* represent the views of the authors, and not necessarily those of the Editorial Board.

Not the U.S. but the World Rejects Hillary/Obama

EDITORIAL

Not the U.S., but the World Rejects Hillary/Obama

Lyndon H. LaRouche, Jr., addressed the LaRouche PAC Policy Committee in the following terms on Nov. 9.

You can't limit yourself to the United States to understand what has happened. What's happened is that a lot of the world has gotten into this act. Some people who are naive may say it's local, that it's only in the United States or parts of the United States. But that's not true. This development was absolutely international; it was not national, but international in its entire character. Germany was a big factor in it. Vladimir Putin of Russia was a big factor in this situation. So that's the pattern; it's not a local pattern in the United States. U.S. factors have significance, but it's not something you can parcel out under categories; you have to see the larger, total picture. That's evident once we start to treat the economy seriously. In other words, instead of trying to figure out how to get this particular product out in a certain way, and so forth, the point is that you have to start on a global basis. What we're dealing with is on a global basis.

Now this has been the actual condition for some time, but it has not been evident because the people have not categorized these things in the proper way. What they've done, is they've accurately looked for things which they think are important,—and they are important. But the issue that governs here, is international, global. And the area is nothing less than global. What you're looking at, is a breakdown of the entire previously existing pattern of life in the world. And when you see that, then you get the whole picture.

Germany was a big part of it. Bill Clinton, by himself, was a crucial figure in this whole process. He set it up, in part. And so, you've got to look at this thing, not from the standpoint of what is important in this area or not; you've got to look at the overall picture, otherwise you don't get the right answers.

Hillary was dumped globally; everything was essentially a global process. This didn't mean that everybody in the planet is working on this thing on a consistent basis, but Germany, Putin, Russia, Asia, all of these elements and more are in the package. You cannot divide this away from that whole. For example: how did the thing get started. Well, Obama was thrown out. How was he thrown out? Well, it was started by Bill Clinton. Bill Clinton set off the first motion which destroyed the whole business. Therefore, you have to look at the totality of the interaction among elements which are definable as having specific characteristics. You don't try to build up something by collecting predetermined desk-work. Because the first one to do this was Bill Clinton. Bill Clinton was the one who sent his wife into the garbage-pail, which is exactly where she belonged. But all these other cases depend upon those kinds of characteristics, and that's the way you have to think of it, not in terms of what the difference is among different states or different areas, and so forth. As in Germany; Germany moved in in a big way, immediately. Key figures in Germany were laying down the law to this effect. Some were not responding, but most of them were.

Putin was a key figure. The entirety of Asia was key. So, the whole thing is something that's acting together, not as a a collection, not as group by group; not state-by-state.

We have to get a new conception of citizenship in the U.S. What we've been operating on were ideas which were never right, throughout the 21st Century to date. What we've just learned now, implicitly globally: China, Russia and so forth: we are all part of one process, and they are not differentiated from the process as such. You have different shadings, as it were, but not different kinds of organization.

The difference now, is that we've been living on illusions,— on assumptions which are actually illusions. We now are pushing into the planet as a whole, and you're going to find that the developing universe is going to be a process. And it will at least be the Earth as part of the universe, and that is going to become very apparent as being a leading factor, which defines the way that all kinds of things, of social relationships, have to be seen together.

What are China's policies? What are the interactions of Asia? Do they divide different sections? What you thought was separate is not. Only the dirty people are separate. All the good people are human, and proud of it.

We're going to have to learn something which lies underneath our noses, so to speak. We are going to take into account factors which you should have been able to recognize, but did not. For example, what's the connection among nations in general? We make too much division, and therefore lose the idea of the whole. And this also affects nations, because nations get these kinds of snotty little self-conscious issues. We are suddenly confronted with—as of now, in fact, in a sense—that we are responsible for humanity,—not merely on Earth. And these things are going to have to come fast.

The assumptions we have made about nations were wrong. They were wrong because they didn't understand humanity. Now, we've got to change it. And we've got change in Germany—very good change. Putin—very good on this; he's already on the case. And the different parts of Asia are working, implicitly, in that direction. But what happens is, you get people who become smug, and think that they have some special control over the identity of other people. The thing is,— yes, there are apparently differences. But, when it comes to understanding what a human being is, that's where people make dirty mistakes. Mankind, mankind in the immediate Universe, is a whole. And you've got to learn that,— you'd better learn it fast.

We'll get unity among human beings as human beings, not by labels on them. They're all human beings. And that's the objective we have to shoot for.

What's going to happen, is this Nazi operation in Ukraine,— we're going to have to eliminate that fact. Other things have to be cleaned out. The point is, what we're looking at is mankind. We're looking at mankind in a universal way, not a particular way, but a universal way. And we're going to learn how to apply our minds. Because most people who are practical people, do not understand their own minds. You have to see yourself in a larger picture, and see your existence in a larger way than most people have ever done.

But this is essential. And what happened on this election day—that is the lesson primarily to be learned. Don't try to break it down!

My wife Helga and I have spent most of our adult lives on a global basis. I've been involved in loyalty to different kinds of nations, to working with them; Helga's done pretty much the same kind of thing. That is the expression, or typification, of what mankind must become. That's what makes mankind human.

The problem in general, is that there's too much emphasis on distinction of type. That's a mistake. Because it does not get to the truth of the matter. What it does, is it selects a target,— "Oh, I like this one; I like this one,"—all at the same time. They don't see what lies in the mind of a child,—even a simple child,—they don't see it. They see what their prejudice has picked out for them. They picked it out! They didn't realize that. Now Helga and I spent most of our lives,—you have to see mankind as in the Universe. And you have to think of mankind living in the Universe of mankind. Einstein's image, in his last years, was close to that. And that's the kind of thing we've got to shoot for, for all mankind. Because we're not going to just be on planet Earth. Mankind is going to develop in nearby space and beyond. And that's the solution to what we have to do. That's exactly what we're shooting for.

I would say that the Einstein position, as Einstein defined himself in the last period of his life—that that's the closest thing you get to what we want to get to. Because you want to get into the Universe. And mankind in the Universe; living in the Universe; developing the Universe. And seeing beyond what we call now the Universe. Because that is what actually defines, fully, the meaning of human life. The usual, "I like this; I like that,"—that's all nonsense. What's important, as Einstein did this very well, in approximation—mankind is there. Mankind is living in the Universe. Mankind acts on the Universe, within the Universe. And therefore mankind avoids particularism. Avoids it. Because your mind has to be developed in full. You've got to think about the Universe. You've got to think of human life, living at a great distance, in some location. That's what you're looking for. You want to see what the role is of mankind in the Universe, as Einstein did, in his own way.

For many people, the "soul" means something at the bottom of a shoe. But mankind, with its development, reaches out into space to see mankind in a broader light,— the way Einstein did in some of his work. That's it! You're going to develop and extend the power of mankind in the Universe, and for the Universe. The time has come to get human beings to think in those terms, now. Because if you don't do that, you will fail. So therefore, you have to have the sense that you are a Universal personality, reaching into space, reaching into areas of development of mankind, beyond what mankind has ever done before. That's the point.

What's your purpose in life? Your purpose in life is to reach beyond what mankind has reached before.

We've made a big mistake by being practical.

Krafft Ehricke, the late, great space scientist, is ac-tually a very useful memory for us, to see exactly what humanity means. And you operate on the basis of fulfilling what that means. And the time has come to do just that.

For me, it's commonplace. Most people tend to be more parochial, and by being more parochial, they become a little bit unpleasant. But the point is, mankind has to live for all mankind. You will understand this by beginning to do it. It's not so hard to understand,—you just have to give up a few favorite hobby-horses.

You can work to that objective; you're going to have to have a determination that you're going to develop yourself in terms of the objective. And bring people to a view of a broader objective for themselves.

EIRContents

www.larouchepub.com Volume 43, Number 46, November 11, 2016

NASA

Cover This Week

The Earth at night, from the International Space Station.

I. Four New Laws

The Four Laws of LaRouche and Hamilton

by Jason Ross

Adapted from a Friday, Nov. 4 webcast; see https:// www.youtube.com/watch?v=9XPBwWs84Go

I've put together a few aids to thinking about what the implementation of LaRouche's Four Laws (http:// larouchepub.com/lar/2014/4124four_laws.html) looks like. In discussing that, I also want to think about this in terms of Hamilton. I'm very happy to say that Hamilton's four great economic writings, along with the Four Laws of Lyndon LaRouche, will be available on Amazon *very soon*. It's been submitted. It should only be a few more days. [Now available on Amazon as *The Vision of Hamilton* (Kindle edition).] I'll be reading some quotes from this.

Let's take a look at what an economic recovery would look like, using LaRouche's Four Laws. Let me read what LaRouche said the remedy to the current situation is. LaRouche writes,

"The only location for the immediately necessary action which could prevent such an immediate genocide throughout the trans-Atlantic sector of the planet, requires the U.S. government's now immediate decision to institute four specific cardinal measures — measures which must be fully consistent with the specific intent of the original U.S. Federal Constitution, as had been specified by U.S. Treasury Secretary Alexander Hamilton while in office. (1) Immediate re-enactment of the Glass-Steagall Law, instituted by U.S. President Franklin D. Roosevelt, without modification as to principle of action. (2) A return to a system of top-down, thoroughly defined national banking." Skipping ahead: "(3) The purpose of the use of a federal credit system, is to generate high productivity trends in improvements in employment, with the accompanying intention to increase the physical economic productivity and standard of living of the persons and households of the United States." And (4), LaRouche writes, "Adopt a fusion-driver 'crash program.' The essential distinction of man from all lower forms of life, is that it presents the means for the perfection of the specifically affirmative aims and needs of the human individual and social life."

Let's take a look through some of these Four Laws. The first step is Glass-Steagall, which I'll just say a little bit about. This is something we've discussed frequently and to great effect, I think, in our programs and on our website.

Take a look here. [**Fig. 1**] This is what percent of

FIGURE 1

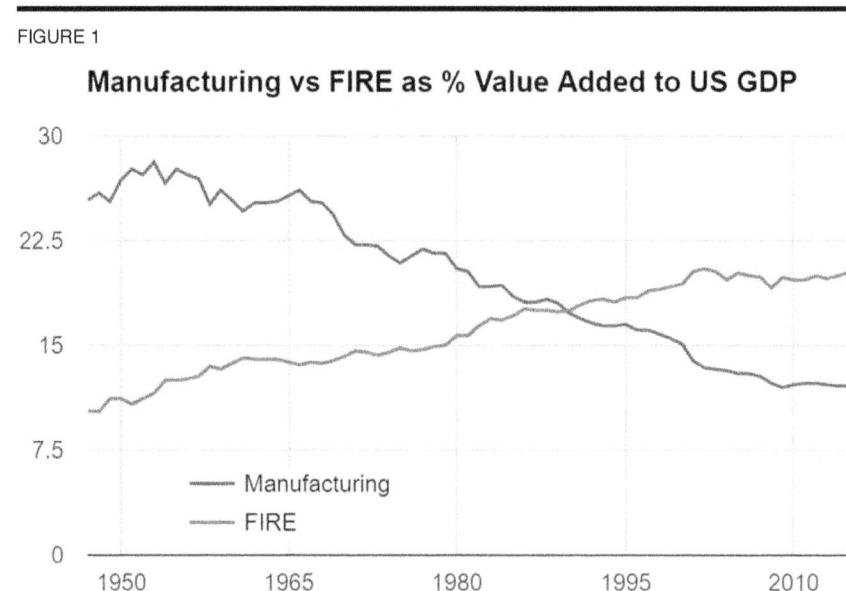

Manufacturing vs FIRE as % Value Added to US GDP

FIGURE 2

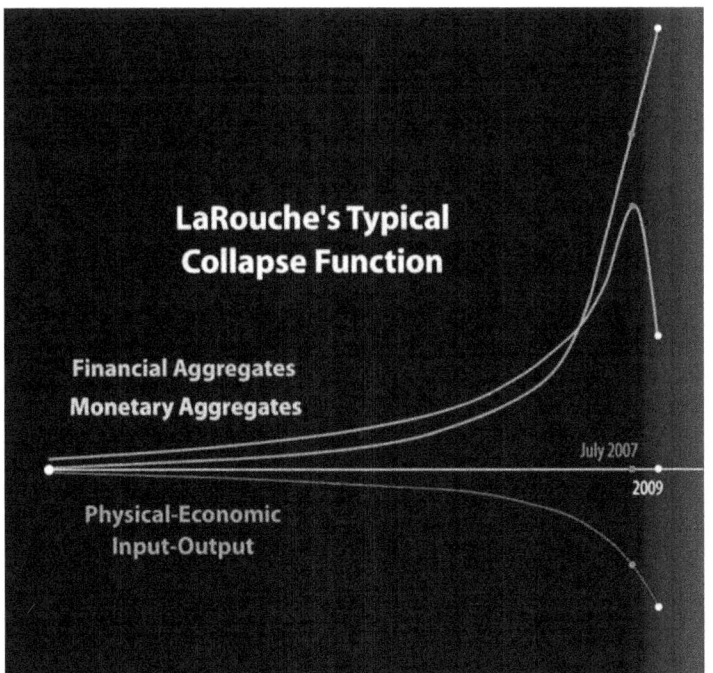

supposed U.S. income, what percent of the value added in our GDP, comes from manufacturing—you see that there in blue—vs. "F.I.R.E.," which stands for finance, insurance, and real estate. For over 30 years now, the world of finance itself has *supposedly*, according to official thinking, contributed as much to U.S. productivity and economy, as has manufacturing. Flipping houses —that kind of thing—is now as productive as manufacturing steel, or building things. It's crazy!

Over this period, [**Fig. 2**]—this is Lyndon La-Rouche's Triple Curve, a pedagogical device that he had used to describe the increase in monetary and financial aggregates, at the same time that the *physical* economic output of the economy was collapsing— we've been in this situation for decades now.

What we need to do, then, is make it *possible* to be able to finance a recovery. Alexander Hamilton, in his reports on public credit and the national bank and on its constitutionality, describes the importance of banking. Banks can provide an essential function for the economy. They're not optional. They provide an essential useful function. Now, they're tied up, in a way, where the potential of the banking sector is impossible right now, because they're involved in all sorts of speculation and gambling. By implementing Glass-Steagall, we make it possible for the banking sector to be able to play that useful role, while jailing and shutting down all

of the people behind the collapse that's been created and the looting that's been taking place via Wall Street.

We've got a lot of very good recent additions to our website. The Economics Frequently Asked Questions page at larouchepac.com/econ-faqs. This addresses some of these questions that come up that *you* may have heard when talking to people about these things. For example: "If Glass-Steagall were still law, it wouldn't have stopped the crash of 2007-8." Are you sick of hearing that? Well, you can now just send people the explanations here. You don't really need to waste your time with it. It's very clear.

National Banking

So, Glass-Steagall's the first step. Step two that Mr. LaRouche describes is national banking. This is definitely a more complex concept. I direct people again, to the works of Alexander Hamilton on this, to get a sense from the beginning, of what it meant to have a national bank, or the role that banking could play in the nation. I'd point to the success of this approach under the administrations of Washington and Hamilton, of John Quincy Adams, of Lincoln, and of Franklin Roosevelt, who, in various ways, created the effect, if not the form, of national banking, through a facility for the promotion of credit and directing it in an economy.

One of the most horrific ideas that people have about how economics works, is that you shouldn't try to direct anything; that government should always stay out; that the "invisible hand" does everything in the best possible way. This is something that Hamilton addresses very directly, countering the arguments of Adam Smith's *Wealth of Nations*, for example, in these reports.

Once we decide that we're going to have a national orientation, and actually choose a direction to go, the question then, is how do we direct this credit in the direction of programs that are going to increase the energy-flux density? How then do we understand "energy-flux density?" This is an economics concept that Mr. LaRouche has employed over the years in his understanding of economy.

We have to think about what is the basis of the transformation of the human species, over time, in a way that's uncharacteristic of any other form of life. This chart of "Population Growth Over the Historical Time

FIGURE 3

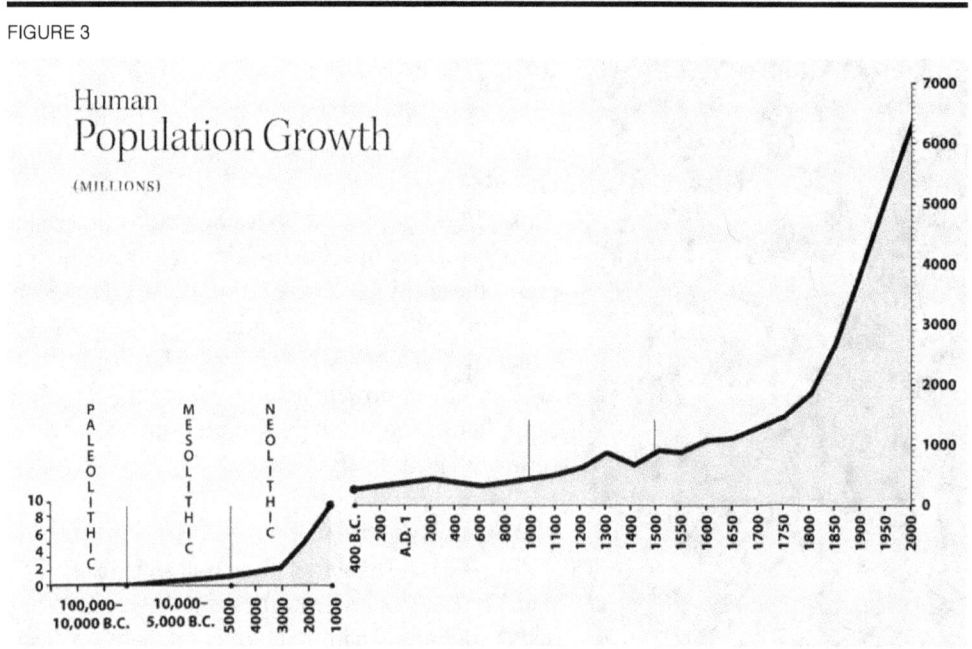

Human
Population Growth
(MILLIONS)

in this original story of the creation of the specifically human species, is this power of fire.

We now consider the different kinds of fire that have been developed over historical time. Take a look at this [**Fig. 4**]. This is the use of different forms of energy over the history of the United States. Two trends we can see here: (1) the energy used per person has, overall, increased—although not at a uniform rate. It's not increasing now. The other thing that we can notice, is that (2) the type of fuel used has changed over time. Wood has very niche applications at present as a fuel. Wood is used for furniture, not for burning. Coal replaced the use of wood, saving forests by making it possible to not have to cut down all sorts of trees to make metals by making charcoal out of the wood. Oil and natural gas supplanted the use of coal. Nuclear fission—which never reached its full potential—in this projection, from the era of the Kennedy administration, was expected to become a primary, dominant form of power for the United States, and, indeed, as seen, for the world.

Period" [**Fig. 3**] is of *human* population growth. It couldn't have been the growth of any animal species acting on its own. Animal species don't transform their relationship to nature. They can't discover principles. They might use a tool, like a stick, to do something, or a rock. They don't use principles as tools.

The beginning of this, the real starting point for this for us historically, certainly in Europe, or extended European civilization, is Prometheus, the Greek story of Prometheus—who really created humanity. Before Prometheus, who, as the story goes, took fire from heaven and gave it to mankind—human beings were animals. Prometheus describes that when he saw mankind, we were just animals. We had eyes to see (but we didn't understand); we had ears, but we didn't understand anything. We lived like swarming ants. What did Prometheus do? He brought fire; he brought astronomy; he brought navigation; he brought beasts of burden; he brought sailing; he brought agriculture; he brought the calendar; he brought poetry; and he brought written language, mathematics, science, knowledge, and fire. What defines us as a species, as

FIGURE 4

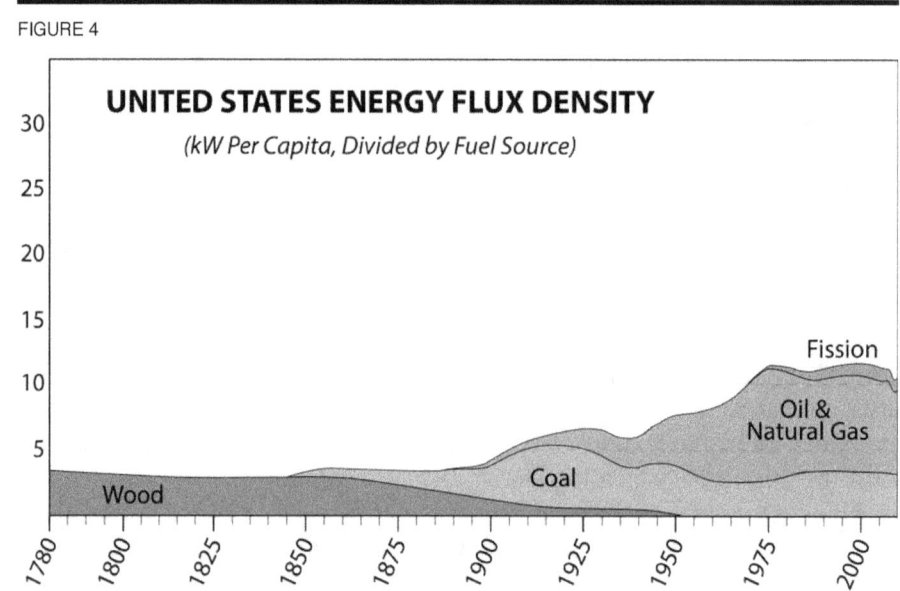

UNITED STATES ENERGY FLUX DENSITY
(kW Per Capita, Divided by Fuel Source)

FIGURE 5

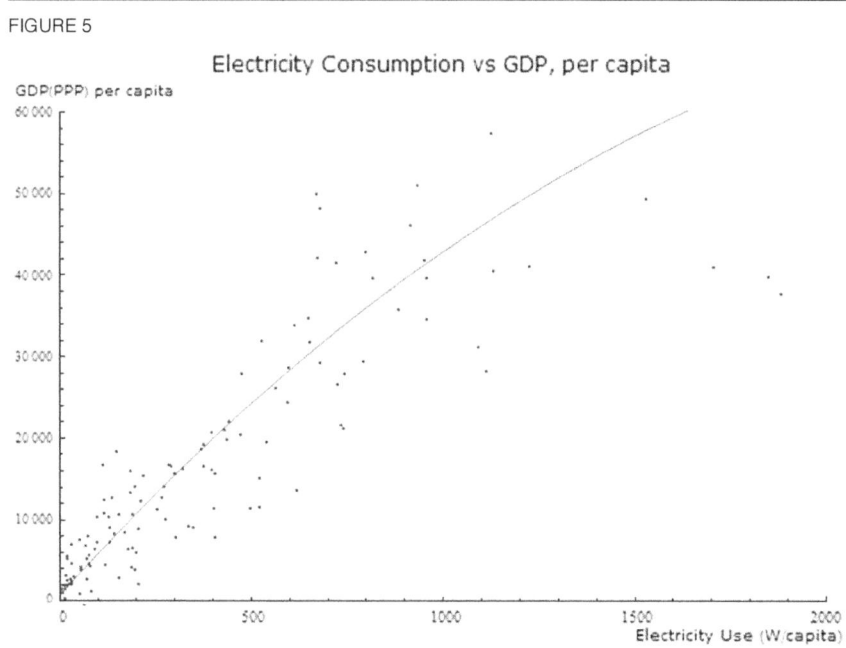

Electricity Consumption vs GDP, per capita

GDP(PPP) per capita

Electricity Use (W/capita)

chart [**Fig. 5**] of electricity use per capita vs. GDP per capita. I know GDP per capita is not the best measure, but it's very clear what you see with these things. If you say, which parts of the world seen here are relatively wealthy and have higher living standards and life expectancies? Well, it's the places where you see the most light. The places where it's dark, that's not because people are people are fond of astronomy in that region and keep their lights off at night so that they can see the stars better. It's because there's not development.

Infrastructure itself really serves as the mediator, the great mediator, of higher forms of energy-flux density into the economy as a whole— the mediator of bringing new technologies into achieving a maximal expression in the economy, by partaking in almost all of the processes that go on in an economy.

The New Silk Road

What this shows us, is, yes, using *more* energy. The other thing is the *type* of energy. What can you do with that energy? Think about what you can do with oil and natural gas that you can't do with coal or wood. You can't run a car with wood. You can't run a car with coal. You can run a car on oil. You can't run a train on wood! You can run a train on coal. What can we do with nuclear power that we can't do with lower forms? Think about how with coal, we can use wood for furniture instead of for burning. Oil: that's what we make plastic out of. Oil is a useful substance. It's a wonderful material. It's a great source of carbon, which, by its chemical nature, is able to form *enormous* molecules. Here it is, sitting in the ground, ready to be used to make all sorts of products, and we're burning it! It's, you know, it's stupid!

With the potential that we've got of shifting to a real nuclear economy, of developing fusion, we would be reaching another stage of energy-flux density. What's the power, the throughput power of your energy source? And what qualitative improvements does it bring? What new things does it allow you to do?

You can't have economic development without power, without energy. Here's a

We now consider the fourth of Mr. LaRouche's Four Laws, which is the call for a crash program on nuclear fusion. This [**Fig. 6**] is a chart that was created back in 1976. What this chart showed was, based on how much money was devoted to achieving the fusion breakthrough, at what year it was anticipated that the great breakthrough for a commercial fusion reactor would

FIGURE 6

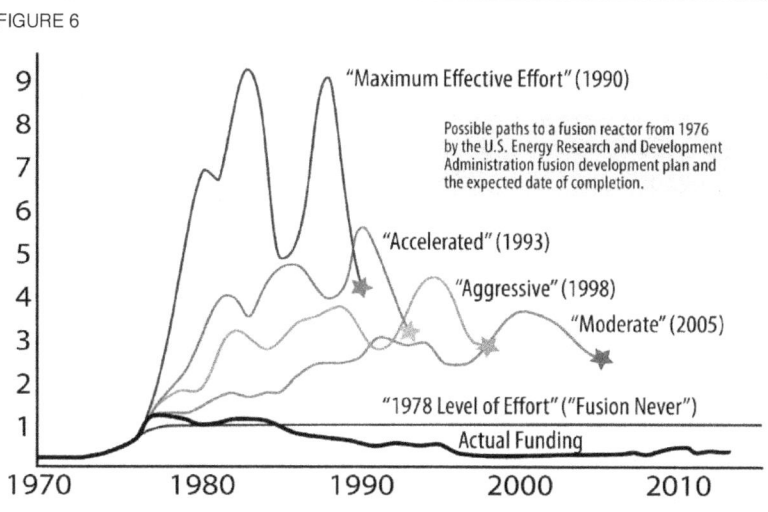

"Maximum Effective Effort" (1990)

Possible paths to a fusion reactor from 1976 by the U.S. Energy Research and Development Administration fusion development plan and the expected date of completion.

"Accelerated" (1993)

"Aggressive" (1998)

"Moderate" (2005)

"1978 Level of Effort" ("Fusion Never")

Actual Funding

Credit: graphic design by Geoffrey M. Olynyk, incorporating 1976 projections from the U.S. Energy Research and Development Administration, "Fusion power by magnetic confinement Program Plan," by S. O. Dean.

FIGURE 7

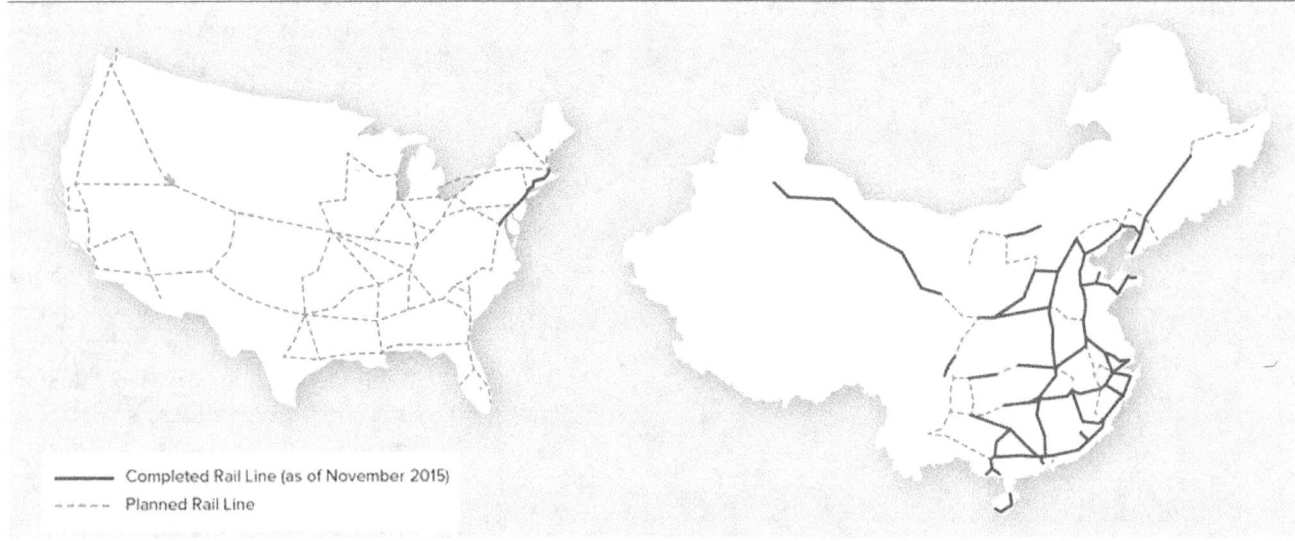

——— Completed Rail Line (as of November 2015)
- - - - - Planned Rail Line

take place. In '76 it was considered that if a maximum possible effort were put into this—something on the scale of the Manhattan Project, or the Apollo Project to go to the Moon—if we took that approach with fusion, it was anticipated that we would have had it over 25 years ago! Even at a moderate level of funding, we should have had it a decade ago, according to this projection, which isn't necessarily exactly right. Actual funding for fusion has been *below the level* that was anticipated in the '70s to *never achieve fusion*. In other words, there has been a decision not to reach the next level of Promethean fire, not to make that breakthrough on fusion.

Why would that happen? Who would hold back the development of fusion power? Is it the oil industry trying to make money selling more oil? No; that is far too simplistic. It is the brutish outlook of the British Empire, of Zeus earlier—Zeus, the character from the Prometheus story. Zeus, the tyrannical god who created his own power in part by holding back others. Preventing mankind from making this step, is one of the greatest crimes that has ever been committed; the deliberate underfunding of fusion and the campaign to prevent its development.

I don't want to go on forever; let me just show a few projects that the United States ought to participate in with a sane outlook. There's a different paradigm going on in the world right now, with the BRICS highly representing this; it represents the decades of work by La-Rouche and the LaRouche movement organizing for this World Land-Bridge proposal, something that's been promoted for decades now. This proposal, the power of this idea to change the world, is absolutely being realized at present. This concept that Lyndon and Helga LaRouche have been organizing for, is now Chinese policy; the "One Belt, One Road" program that is now bringing together over 70 nations representing the majority of the world's population. The greatest potential for economic growth in the world; this is a policy that is taking place.

What the U.S.A. Could Be

Instead, the United States under Obama—who should be thrown out of office yesterday, if not last week, last month, last year; those would all be even better—is holding these things back. What would it look like if we joined? One thing would be the Bering Strait crossing, a proposal that was first discussed over a century ago. Really bringing the United States, via land, into coordination and connection with Eurasia and Africa, with the rest of the world in a very serious way, a new way and a more efficient way than sea-borne shipping. Within the United States, we've got [**Fig. 7**] to test your geography here, this is the United States on the left, and on the right that is China. Similar nations in size. Look at all that high-speed rail in China that you see in blue, and probably some of the red; since this map was made, they've probably completed it, they're building it so rapidly. The United States doesn't have a high-speed rail network; we barely have a rail network. Instead, we use the less-efficient form of road transportation for freight and for people stuck in traffic jams. What would it mean to build a network that makes the United States more efficient, more productive? How many jobs would be involved in building new cities, in building the kinds of power plants that would be required? What kind of power could we have over our physical economy with the really full development of control over the water cycle? It is within our means to create desalination right now in California to provide for coastal water needs if we wanted to do that. It's within our ability to do serious and in-depth research on atmospheric ionization and other technologies to control the water cycle. It's within our ability to transfer water that has already fallen on land; but we need to ensure that there's actually enough to make that a possibility.

So, let me read a couple of quotes from Alexander Hamilton here, in terms of where an understanding of an increase in energy flux density, of where economic growth comes from. It doesn't come from money; it comes from the human mind. Here's Treasury Secretary Hamilton. He's describing in the beginning of his "Report on Manufactures" whether it makes sense to have a manufacturing economy, as opposed to a purely agricultural one, which today seems like a stupid argument to even have, but it was something that Thomas Jefferson didn't get, for example. Because he wanted to keep the American economy from developing; he didn't have that same outlook on human beings—clearly—that Alexander Hamilton did.

So, Hamilton writes that "the work of artificers as opposed to cultivators," that is, manufacturing as opposed to farming, "is susceptible of a greater improvement in a proportionately greater degree of improvement of its productive powers; whether by the accession of skill, or from the application of ingenious machinery"—labor saving machinery. How does the development of a new technology transform the potential of production in an economy? This is a quote Matt had used: Hamilton writes—on page 148 when you get the book—"It merits particular observation that the multiplication of manufactories not only furnishes a market for those articles which have been accustomed to be produced in abundance in a country, but it likewise creates a demand for such as were either unknown or produced in inconsiderable quantities. The bowels as well as the surface of the Earth are ransacked for articles which were before neglected. Animals, plants, and minerals acquire a utility and value which were before unexplored." Iron ore wasn't iron ore before the Iron Age; it was a rock. Malachite wasn't copper ore before the Bronze Age; it was just a green rock that Egyptians used for mascara. You transform the value of the things around you; the mind transforms what those things are. That rock was transformed into ore by the human mind. We change the universe through our discoveries; we transform our relationship to it, we change what it is, what it can participate in.

Hamilton understood that the purpose of the United States was nothing less than the promotion of the General Welfare. This quote is a bit long to read, but it's on page 187; and it's where he describes that there shouldn't be a limitation—except what comes up in the Constitution—against government action to promote the General Welfare. He says "the term General Welfare, doubtless intended to signify more than was expressed or imported in those parts of the Constitution and Congress' powers which preceded it. This phrase is as comprehensive as any that could have been used, because it was not fit that the Constitutional authority of the Union to appropriate its revenues should have been restricted within narrower limits than the General Welfare." The real point to take is that it's a different economic outlook. What China is doing is great, but it's not up to the level of what it should be. The concept embodied in the One Belt, One Road project is positive; it's very good. But what really needs to be brought to this, is the explicit understanding of its basis in the human identity. The human ability to make discoveries that transform our relationship to Nature; that's the key to economics. We see its effects in various studies we might do about how building a road transforms the amount of agricultural production in an area; or how bringing in a stable power supply allows factories not to have to turn off every three hours when the power goes out—what transformations that makes. But the real key is to give a mission to people, by participation in the ability to bring that to a yet higher level of understanding, of living standards, and of participation in that process. That's the key thing; to create a society where people are able to participate knowingly in that increase.

Restore Our National Mission for Scientific Progress

by Kesha Rogers, former U.S. Senate Candidate in Texas

Nov. 2—Lyndon LaRouche has defined the standard for economic progress, and the measures urgently needed today to free the United States and the world from the grip of a total dark age culture of death and despair, to one that develops the greatest creative potential of every person living. Most importantly, our commitment is to the generations yet to be born. As LaRouche has developed, "The question in terms of economy involves not simply products capable of measurement as such, but rather involves the requirement of developing human minds in new ways that the human mind has ever fashioned to do it."

The measurement of a productive society is not defined by money. Money has no intrinsic value. The measurement of wealth in an economy is understood in what LaRouche describes as physical economic terms; that is, the increase in the productive powers of labor of a society, per capita and per square kilometer. This standard, as defined by the first Treasury Secretary of the United States, Alexander Hamilton, is the founding principle on which Lyndon LaRouche develops his urgently needed Four Laws to save the United States today. The four measures are described here in short:

1. The immediate re-enactment of the Glass-Steagall law instituted by U.S. President Franklin D. Roosevelt, without modification, as to principle of action.

2. A return to a system of top-down, and thoroughly so defined, as National Banking. The precedents for this shall be taken from the banking-and-credit system established by Alexander Hamilton, as well as Abraham Lincoln's action of creating a national currency ("Greenbacks"), under Presidential authority.

3. The deployment of a new Federal Credit system to generate high-productivity trends in improvements of employment, with the accompanying intention to increase the physical-economic productivity, and the standard of living of the persons and households of the United States. An increase in productive employment, as accomplished under Franklin Roosevelt, must reflect an increase in real productivity, coherent with an increase in energy-flux density in the nation's economic practice.

4. The adoption of a Fusion-Energy Driver Crash Program. Real economics is grounded in the essential distinction of Man from all lower forms of life. A Fusion Crash Program, today subsuming a return to Krafft Ehricke's vision for the U.S. Space Program, is a commitment to mankind's future.

Sandia Labs

The center section of Sandia's Z machine for inertial fusion is prepared for each shot.

Hamilton's Principles

The standards set forth by Alexander Hamilton in his four reports to Congress were the principles on which our nation was formed. Hamilton described the essential principle of economy as a system of productivity, where the primary measure of value was not based on capital, but the creative powers of mind that increase the productive powers of labor. Our Nation's Declaration of Independence and Preamble to the Constitution demanded Hamilton's credit system. The idea of the inalienable rights of man is premised on the freedom of human beings to create and discover new principles which improve mankind's existence in and over the universe. The Pursuit of Happiness is not defined by how much money you possess or what a nation holds in its treasury. It is defined by the ability of each person to contribute to the productivity of the nation and the posterity of that nation. This defines the necessity for Credit. Wealth is not created by the printing of money. Wealth is measured in the productivity of the economy.

The universal principles articulated by Hamilton in his four reports define the measures so urgently needed today to bring about a new paradigm throughout the planet. These measures, developed uniquely by LaRouche, are now being adopted by leading nations throughout the world, and must be the standards to which the United States immediately returns.

A nation's commitment to its future, and to increasing the scientific and creative output of its society, is a fundamental principle understood by those leaders who have enacted the standard of credit defined by Alexander Hamilton. The development of space, and of all resources, is a key driver for economic progress throughout the planet. It is not a matter of simply implementing low-cost programs, placing human lives and the destiny of the nation in the hands of profiteers. Space exploration is essential for freeing mankind from the confines of one small planet, ending any limitations to mankind's growth and potential. We must free mankind from the grip of tyranny, of poverty, and of the threat of thermonuclear war which now endangers our very human existence—a result of the failed policies of speculation and bailouts that have continued to dominate the United States and trans-Atlantic system. We must seek to free our nation's people from a culture of degeneracy, drug abuse, death and despair—the lawful product of the Presidencies of George W. Bush and, especially, Barack Obama, now for nearly two decades. A renewed mission for scientific progress is required.

Visionaries of Space Exploration

As President Kennedy and the true visionaries of our space program understood, a national policy for the development of space should be based on the standard of the promotion of a system of national credit, as prescribed by Alexander Hamilton. The space program cannot be seen from the standpoint of a monetary policy, or even a public-private partnership for investors to invest in for some short-term monetary returns or tax write-off perks; it must start from the standpoint of the investigation of the universe and the creative mission of mankind to explore space. This is essential to any economic driver for increasing the productivity of mankind throughout the planet, and throughout the Galaxy. The late, great visionary and space pioneer, Krafft Ehricke, defined this quality of space program based on the increasing need for growth and development of mankind's power over the biosphere and beyond. As he stated:

"Today's mankind can obviously not exist without industrial productivity or without the biosphere, and the activities through technological progress. A mankind which does not grow in technological skills and the quality of industrial productivity, will become an unbearable burden on the biosphere. Declining, or even stagnant technology and industry, are not a viable solution on behalf of mankind or the biosphere."

This is the standard of growth on which nations now adopting the policies of Hamilton and LaRouche are coming together—part of a commitment for cooperation on economic progress—as expressed by the initiatives of Russia and China, as with China's offer of a win-win solution for the benefit of every nation, as prescribed in its Belt and Road policy. This includes the development of space, such as China's commitment to explore the far side of the Moon. The BRICS countries (Brazil, Russia, India, China, South Africa) have continued to defy the intent of the oligarchy to deny a productive future to the people of this world. In a recent speech to the Valdai International Discussion Club in Sochi, Russia, Russian President Vladimir Putin developed this conception:

"We cannot achieve global stability unless we guarantee global economic progress. It is essential to provide conditions for creative labor and economic growth at a pace that would put an end to the division of the world into permanent winners and permanent losers. The rules of the game should give the developing econ-

NASA

The Apollo 11 Saturn V space vehicle lifts off, 16 July 1969.

omies at least a chance to catch up with those we know as developed economies. We should work to level out the pace of economic development, and brace up backward countries and regions so as to make the fruit of economic growth and technological progress accessible to all. Particularly, this would help put an end to poverty, one of the worst contemporary problems."

Putin: Realizing Human Potential

Later, Putin stated, "An important task of ours is to develop human potential. Only a world with ample opportunities for all, with highly skilled workers, access to knowledge, and a great variety of ways to realize their potential, can be considered truly free; only a world where people from different countries do not struggle to survive, but lead full lives, can be stable."

Shortly following this address, member states of the BRICS agreed to set up joint systems of space satellites for Earth remote sensing, as reported by the head of the Russian space corporation Roscosmos. This is a decisive move toward cooperation in space, one which leaves the United States isolated. The commitment to cooperation in the development of space by those nations which are joining with Russia and China, falls directly in line with the vision set forth by Krafft Ehricke as he describes the concept of space travel:

"The concept of space travel carries with it enormous impact, because it challenges Man on practically all fronts of his physical and spiritual existence. The idea of travelling to other celestial bodies reflects to the highest degree the independence and agility of the human mind. It lends ultimate dignity to Man's technical and scientific endeavors. Above all, it touches on the philosophy of his very existence. As a result, the concept of space travel disregards national borders, refuses to recognize differences of historical and ethnological origin, and penetrates the fiber of one sociological and political creed as fast as that of the next."

A National Mission

We must restore our commitment once again to a national mission and a true science-driver program as LaRouche has mandated in his Four Laws. The United States must take up the offer of international cooperation. We must define a new standard of credit for development throughout the planet, just as Hamilton established—one which supersedes mere monetary value and establishes a system that truly invests in the future of our people and the future of our nation.

China's Space Program: A Treasure for Mankind

by Megan Beets

[Chang'e-4 is] a breakthrough in human history.

—Ouyang Zhiyuan, Founder of the Chinese Lunar Program

Now more than ever, the people of the United States are ready for a universal change—ready to soundly reject the failed and deadly policies of the past two presidents, and to crush the Wall Street swindlers who have literally gotten away with murder.

It is urgent that U.S. citizens demand a return to the *valid* notion of economic value advanced by two of the greatest geniuses in history, Lyndon LaRouche[1] and Alexander Hamilton.[2] As found in their respective writings, the only true standard of economic value is whether or not an activity within the economy contributes to an increasing development of the creative powers of the minds of the population, for which that economy exists.

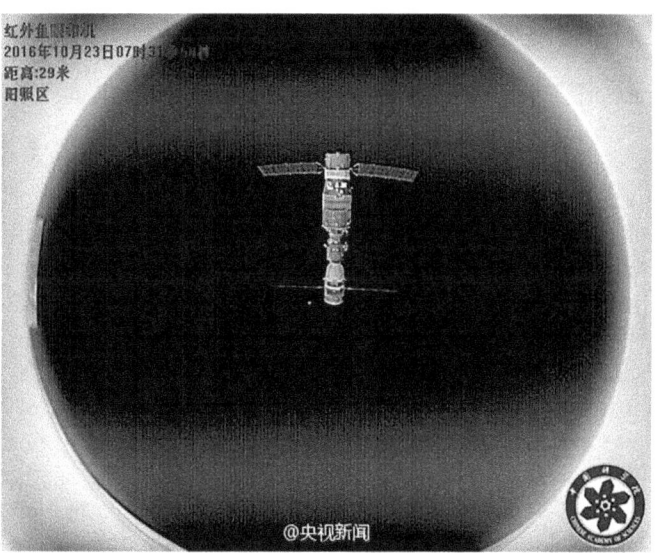

红外监视图讯
2016年10月23日07时31
距高:29米
阳眠区

@央视新闻

english.cri.cn

The first selfie of Shenzhou-11 docked with Tiangong-2, taken by a satellite launched from Tiangong-2.

The leading expression of that principle today is *not* found in the United States or Europe—but in China, as it commits its rapidly progressing space program to breaking the boundaries of planet Earth and moving mankind to the far side of the Moon. It has invited the United States, and all nations, to join them.

China's Extraterrestrial Commitment

In 2018, a Chinese lander will touch down on the far side of the Moon—a place that has never seen, on its surface, the presence of mankind, either human or robotic. The lander will deploy a small rover to explore the landing site, one of the largest impact craters in the solar system,[3] and together with the rover and a relay satellite parked in orbit behind the Moon, will take the very first pictures of our universe in the very-low-frequency (VLF) radio range. This lunar far side mission, Chang'e-4, will change mankind forever, as it opens the potential to fully unlock the Moon's secrets, and to take the preliminary steps to establish mankind as a polyglobal species.

Over the next two years, leading up to that great achievement, China plans an ambitious series of missions, some of which are already underway.

In 2017, the Chang'e-5 lander will be the first spacecraft since 1976 to travel to the Moon and return, bringing lunar samples back to Earth. Ouyang Zhiyuan, father of China's lunar program, assured that "We are ready. Every lab is ready [to receive the samples]. Once the samples are back, we can begin our analysis right away." In 2018, China will put the first components of its full-size space station into orbit, and construction is expected to be finished in 2022.

---

1. "The Four New Laws to Save the U.S.A. Now! Not an Option: An Immediate Necessity," http://www.larouchepac.com/four-laws/.
2. See Hamilton's four reports to Congress, https://larouchepac.com/20161013/alexander-hamiltons-four-economic-papers/. They are also available on Kindle as *The Vision of Hamilton: Hamilton's 4 Reports and LaRouche's 4 Laws*.
3. The South Pole-Aitkin Basin is an intriguing landing site. Among other interesting features, the exposed terrain is from deep geological layers, giving us a chance to see far into the Moon's past.

Three important precursors to these missions were launched earlier this autumn.

The Tiangong-2 space lab[4] was put into orbit around Earth on September 15. One month later, Tiangong-2 was joined by the Shenzhou-11 spacecraft, China's sixth manned mission, which carried two taikonauts and is currently docked with the space lab for a 30-day stay in space—the longest yet of any Chinese crew.

On November 3, the launchpad at the recently completed Wenchang Launch Center roared to life as China carried out the first test launch of the heavy-lift Long March 5 rocket. The successful launch of the Long March 5 was a crucial step for the success of upcoming missions, which require the Long March 5's larger capacity.[5]

Other missions on the horizon are a lander and rover on Mars, slated for 2020, and an orbiter around Venus for the mid-2020s. And there is a clear trajectory toward manned missions to the Moon, once the success of the robotic missions is secured.

New Silk Road into Space

China has extended the win-win principle of the New Silk Road beyond cooperation on Earth, inviting all UN member countries to participate in China's space station.[6] "Space exploration is the common dream and wish of humankind. We believe that the implementation of the agreements will definitely promote international cooperation on space exploration, and create opportunities for United Nations Member States, particularly developing countries, to take part in, and benefit from, the utilization of China's space station," said General Wu Ping, Deputy Director of the China Manned Space Agency.

China has also invited all other nations to make use of the communications relay satellite that will be launched as part of the Chang'e-4 far side mission, "for supporting future manned and unmanned lunar exploration missions to the far side, and cislunar activities."[7]

Other nations are eager for this cooperation![8] The European Space Agency, for example, is having its astronauts study Chinese, and European nations have provided four of the instruments on the Chang'e-4 far side mission. Also significant in this regard is the first meeting, held November 2, of representatives from the space agencies of the five BRICS nations. This begins a process of integrating and coordinating the assets and capabilities of these countries for space exploration.

Several of the nations involved in the burgeoning new paradigm in Eurasia have missions to the Moon planned for the next five years, including India, Russia, Japan, and Korea.[9] All of these nations express excitement for the progress of their own nations, and for mankind as a whole, toward a new capability of humanity in space.

A New, Human Standard

As we in the United States experienced during the 1960s, the space program is the driver for advances in mankind's capabilities beyond what would be possible as merely a resident of Earth. The space program not only drove advances in technologies, but set an intellectual and moral standard within the nation. It pushed the boundaries of our limitations into realms that were never thought of before. It began to remake man as a more powerful species than ever before. A reflection of this was the upward leaps in economic productivity that resulted from the introduction of completely new kinds of technologies and materials into industrial and other processes.

That process was not something particular to that time in the United States. It is always the advance of the creative human mind beyond what we knew or could have known in the past that drives our progress as a species, and hence, the economy. Today, China, with its space program, is leading the rest of the world in opening the door, once again, for great achievements of this nature. It is high time for the people of the United States to return to our principles, and join China—to dump the system of Obama and Wall Street, and to revive our space program as the leading driver of economic progress today.

---

4. Tiangong-2 will be the final phase of the proto-space station, as China now has the confidence to move forward with a full-size, long-stay station.

5. The Long March 5 has a payload capacity of 25 tons to low earth orbit, and 8 tons to translunar orbit. The next generation, Long March 9, will be able to carry payloads comparable to NASA's long lost Saturn V.

6. If the International Space Station is indeed decommissioned in the mid-2020s, the Chinese space station will be the only game in town.

7. Wu Yanhua, vice administrator of China's National Space Administration, on Sept. 26, 2016 at the International Astronautical Conference in Guadalajara, Mexico.

8. This emphatically includes the scientific community in the United States. However, a juvenile and morally irresponsible ban on collaboration between NASA and anybody associated with the Chinese Space Agency has prevented such cooperative efforts. This ban must be overturned immediately—and its enforcers in Congress relocated to the nearest retirement community.

9. The four planned missions to the Moon are—India: Chandrayan-2; Russia: Luna 25-28, in cooperation with the European Space Agency; Japan: Smart Lander for Investigating Moon (SLIM); and the Korean Pathfinder Lunar Orbiter (KPLO).

Long March Launch Takes China's Aerospace Technology to a New Platform

by Marsha Freeman

Nov. 6—On November 3, China conducted the test launch of its new Long March 5 rocket. It was a complete success. Liftoff took place at 8:43 PM local time (8:43 AM EDT), and the payload was successfully placed in a predetermined orbit. But the importance of this launch was not to deliver a payload, but to test the results of more than a decade of research and development of a new family of technologies which, in addition to enabling the next-generation lunar and manned missions, and China's first foray into interplanetary space, will increase productivity throughout the economy. Meng Fanxin, a manager in the Tianjin branch of China Aerospace Science and Technology Corp., which built the Long March 5, pointed to this on the day of the launch: "The rocket is a big step forward, not only for China's aerospace industry, but [it] will also boost the development of the country's whole industrial system."

Chinese economists, scientists and engineers, and scholars have studied the historical precedent—the impact of the Apollo program on the U.S. economy. The economic benefit of the Apollo program is most often measured in dollar terms, on the order of a 10:1 return on investment. But what the investment in the American lunar program created, was entirely new technologies in order to meet the challenge of putting men into space. Applied later in manufacturing, agriculture, medicine, transportation, communications, and almost every field of human endeavor, the technological transformation of the U.S. economy through the applications of space technologies was the driver of economic growth for more than a decade after the lunar landings were accomplished. The longest-lasting contribution of the Apollo program was the generations of young people who became scientists and engineers, inspired by space exploration, and the optimism that they could contribute to creating the future.

Since the 1970s, China has used a family of Long March rockets that has seen incremental improvements in payload capacity and other factors over the

China National Space Administration

The Long March 5 rocket at the launch pad.

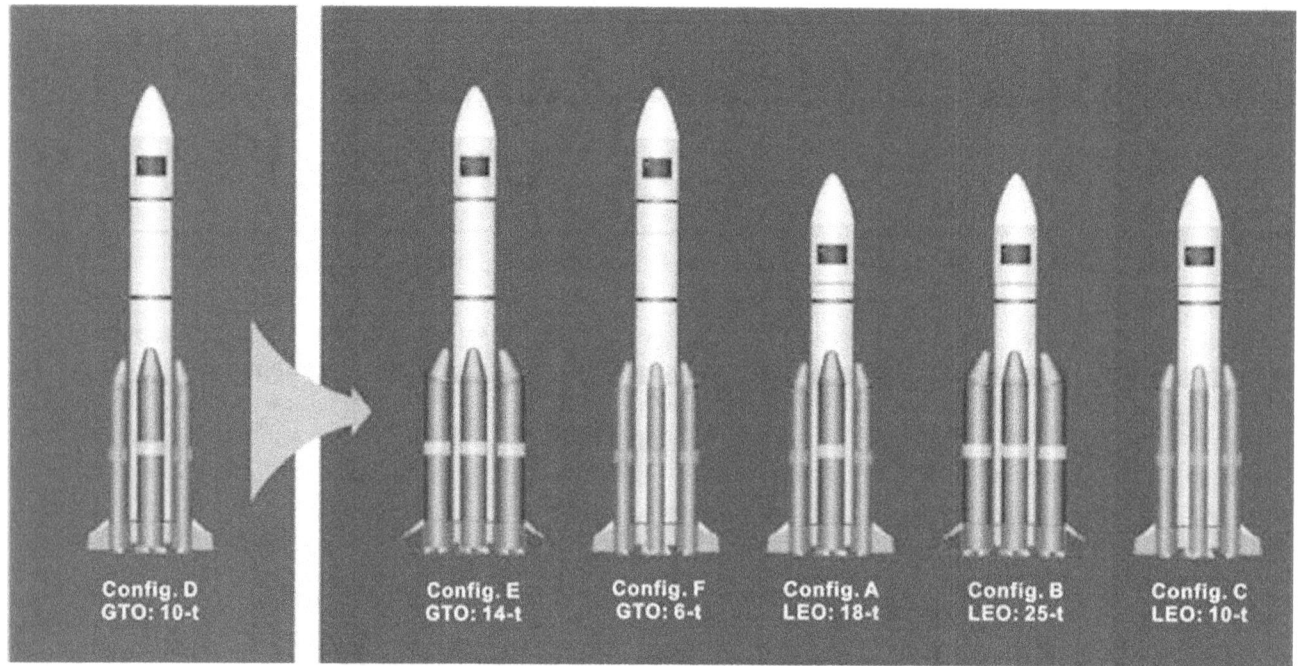

Configurations of the Long March 5 rocket, showing payload tonnages and destinations (geostationary transfer orbit and low Earth orbit).

decades. But to take the next steps in its manned exploration, with a space station, the challenging lunar sample return and far-side missions, and its first planetary exploration mission to Mars, an entirely new class of launch vehicles is required. The Long March 5, with its ability to deliver a 25-ton payload into low Earth orbit, and place about 14 tons of payload in a transfer orbit to the Moon, now places China in a league comparable to that of the U.S., Russia, and Europe.

The Long March 5 is not an incremental improvement over earlier versions, but a leap in technology, with a payload capacity two-and-half times that of China's existing fleet. This dramatic increase required a complete redesign of the rocket, the development of new materials, the creation of a new launch center and of the processes for carrying out much more complex missions. The new rocket, "is not just a simple enlargement of the diameter [of the rocket]," explained Lou Luliang, a designer from China's State Administration of Science, Technology and Industry for National Defense after the launch. "It raised new requirements of materials, manufacturing, and equipment." He added that components from the new rocket would be retrofitted to older Long March vehicles.

Professor Yang Yuguang, from the Beijing Institute of Electronic Systems Engineering of the China Aerospace Science and Industry Corp., explains that the Long March 5 adopted a larger, 5 meter diameter for its core stage, as compared to the 3.35 meter diameter Long March 2 series, which just weeks earlier had taken a two-man Shenzhou-11 crew into orbit. The larger rocket raised the requirement for the rigidity of the core, because of the increased stress of aerodynamic forces. In order to manufacture the new core stage, Dr. Yang explains, new welding technology was adopted. "Generally speaking," he reports, "spacecraft manufacturing always has higher requirements for welding procedures than other industry."

The new welding technique, he says, can be transferred to other industrial fields, and "benefit daily life." An interesting application that Dr. Yang mentions, is the adoption of these welding techniques from the spacecraft manufacturing factory, for new statues that are being built in China. Many industries require very large welded components, such as pressure vessels for fossil fuel and nuclear plants, so there will be many potential applications.

Another example Dr. Yang cites is the fact that the Long March 5 "needs tens of thousands of connecters, fasteners, and other small parts with very special performance requirements. Most of these parts are made of titanium alloy. The processing and manufacture of these titanium alloy parts [required] some special technologies. Similar material-making technologies adopted in the Long March 5 are also widely used in industry," he reports.

When a component produced in a factory is flawed, it is generally discarded and replaced. If a component, or even the smallest part of a rocket malfunctions, it could mean the life of the crew. The Long March 5 "is a completely new rocket," Dr. Yang says. "Almost 100 percent of the technologies it used are being applied for the first time. To ensure the success of its launch, the testing procedure is very critical." The new procedures that were developed for "testing facilities in the ground-support system, both the hardware and software, can be transferred automatically to manufacturing industry," greatly increasing productivity. "Failure-detection and testing for malfunctions can ensure the safety of automated manufacturing processes, and efficiently reduce the cost," says Dr. Yang.

New Space Infrastructure

In order to launch the Long March 5 and the follow-on larger versions, an entirely new launch com-

plex was needed. The larger-diameter core stage could not be transported by rail, as had been the mode until now. The Wenchang launch site, situated on southern Hainan Island, was the ideal location, where rockets of any size could be delivered by ship. Two new specially designed ships, designated Yuanwang 21 and 22, deliver components to the launch center from the factory in the port city of Tianjin. The new factory incorporates the tooling and manufacturing capacity needed for this new family of larger rockets, which will be assembled from modular components. Another advantage of the island launch site, is that falling rocket stages would land in the ocean, and not in villages, as the path of the rocket takes it over water. The more favorable southern latitude also increases the efficiency of each rocket launch. All of these same characteristics account for the Florida location at Cape Canaveral, of the Kennedy Space Center.

The new Hainan Island facility will be for civilian space launches, as distinct from its other launch sites which are used for military payloads. So China has opened up the site to visitors, tourists, and families. Foreign guests were invited to the Nov. 3 Long March 5 launch, which was shown live on television. Educational facilities, a space theme park, and accommodations for both astronauts and visitors are planned for the site. The development of the Long March 5 was approved by the government in 2007, and construction of the new launch site began then.

To increase payload capacity, a safer and more energetic petroleum-based rocket fuel is used in the Long March 5. The new vehicle also includes high-energy liquid hydrogen engines, the largest ever used by China. Using liquid hydrogen for propulsion, which was originally pioneered by the great space scientist Krafft Ehricke, opens up the possibility of more advanced deep-space and planetary missions. The cryogenic liquid hydrogen must be kept at near-zero-degree temperature, requiring handling technologies which can also be used in industry.

As the new materials, technologies, and processes developed for the Long March rocket are "spun off" into industry as well as people's daily lives, Dr. Yang says that "most of the benefits from making the Long March 5 are indirect technological transfers, which we can not see or describe directly. But the whole national economy indeed gets a remarkable return from this project."

Every Day Counts In Today's Showdown To Save Civilization

NEW REDUCED PRICE!

That's why you need EIR's **Daily Alert Service**, a strategic overview compiled with the input of Lyndon LaRouche, and delivered to your email 5 days a week.

For example: On Oct. 28, EIR's Daily Alert highlighted the speech of Russian President Putin at the Valdai Club, where he put forth a series of economic initiatives, arguing that peace cannot be achieved without economic progress. This, despite all the filthy provocations being circulated against Russia in the Western press. Russia wants to cooperate economically as well as against terror.

The same edition also features the latest motion in the U.S. toward Glass-Steagall by, of all people, Donald Trump.

We're not just warning of the real dangers of financial collapse and war. Each edition of EIR Alert points to aspects of the rapid momentum toward sanity worldwide, providing information you need to act on if we are going to survive as a nation and a species. Can you really afford to be without it?

TUESDAY, NOVEMBER 1, 2016
Volume 3, Number 50

EIR Daily Alert Service
P.O. Box 17390, Washington, DC 20041-0390

- Hillary's Plan for Regime Change in Syria Means Nuclear War with Russia
- The Empire's Financial Times Gives 'Kiss of Death' Endorsement to Hillary Clinton
- Another Black Eye for Obama's Pivot to Asia, and War—Malaysia's Najib Visits China
- China, Philippines 'Friendly Understanding' Now Official on Fishing in 'Traditional' Areas
- Fidel Ramos Quits as Philippine Special Envoy to China
- UN's Syria Envoy Charges Jihadists with War Crimes in Eastern Aleppo

EDITORIAL

Hillary's Plan for Regime Change in Syria Means Nuclear War with Russia

Oct. 31 (EIRNS)—One thing that Donald Trump has correct is that

---

Geopolitics on Washington's Behalf—Or a Policy for the Common Aims of Mankind?

by Helga Zepp-LaRouche, chairwoman of the German political party Civil Rights Movement Solidarity (BüSo)

Nov. 5—No matter who wins the United States elections this coming Tuesday, every country in the world is going to have to re-evaluate its own strategic situation and fundamental interests, and realign its policies. In the event the hawkish Hillary Clinton wins, Germany's foreign policy will immediately be presented with the challenge of refusing to be drawn into a direct military confrontation between the United States and Russia—a situation Clinton's announced Syrian policy threatens to bring about. If Donald Trump wins, it will be a totally new roll of the dice.

Given this situation, what an opportunity was lost during German Economics Minister Sigmar Gabriel's recent trip to China! Like a well-trained poodle who dutifully attempted to carry out Washington's agenda, Gabriel mutated into the proverbial bull in a china shop during the run-up to the trip and the five days he spent in Beijing, Chengdu, and Hong Kong.

Germany can—still—play a unique role in averting the clearly recognizable imminent catastrophe of a military confrontation between the West, and Russia and China, and in setting a new course toward a positive outcome of the current epoch through deliberate cooperation with the New Silk Road dynamic. But Gabriel basically mucked up this opportunity.

As the business daily *Handelsblatt* pointed out, in the run-up to the trip, the German government, by order of U.S. intelligence services, blocked Chinese in-

vestment in the Aachen firm Aixtron, by revoking the security clearance required for the takeover. Marc Tuengler, chief executive officer of the German Society for the Protection of Securities Holders, which represents the interests of the Aixtron shareholders, reproached Gabriel for harming Germany and carrying out the Obama Administration's dirty work against China. In light of the fact that Aixtron in recent years has delivered many chip-producing machines to China—as did the American competitor firm Veeco, which stands to benefit from this action—the argument

Xinhua/Wang Ye

Chinese Premier Li Keqiang (right) meets with visiting German Vice Chancellor and Minister for Economic Affairs and Energy Sigmar Gabriel in an earlier trip to Beijing, April 2014.

whitehouse.gov

Tobas Koch/OTRS

Olaf Kosinsky/Skillshare.eu

German Economics Minister Sigmar Gabriel is sticking to the anti-China script. Enforcers are (top left) U.S. Treasury's sanctions czar Adam Szubin and (left) EU foreign affairs representative Federica Mogherini.

the enormous political, economic, and social consequences of these sanctions, it is absolutely embarrassing how easily German industry caves in, instead of using its influence with the government.

Minister Gabriel Needs New Glasses

Gabriel did his best, both before and during his China trip, to stick to the anti-Chinese line of the European Union (EU). Thus, he demanded new EU laws and regulations in order to block unwelcome Chinese direct investment in Germany. Daimler head Dieter Zetsche countered him energetically and confronted him with the obvious question: Who should set the criteria for declaring an investor unwelcome—should the government do so, thereby going back to protectionism? China now educates substantially more engineers than Germany does, he said, so the argument that China has to copy our technologies is nonsense.

During his visit to Hong Kong for the conference of the Asia-Pacific Committee of German Industry, Gabriel also carried out the EU policy of using relations with the ASEAN nations as a counterweight to China—a policy defended by EU foreign affairs representative Federica Mogherini.

What goes around comes around. The planned joint opening of a German-Chinese industry event by Gabriel and Chinese Commerce Minister Gao Hucheng was called off, as was his meeting with Reform Commission Chairman Liu He and a joint press conference with Prime Minister Li Keqiang.

The few useful results of the trip lay, and lie, in the fact that the 60-person industrial delegation certainly understands the fundamental advantages of cooperation with China, as well as the indisputable fact that the music of the future in regard to economic and strategic matters is playing in Asia, and no longer in the trans-Atlantic sector.

Gabriel's behavior before and during the trip is almost an object lesson in how—by wearing the glasses of the old, geopolitical paradigm—we, at best, distort and misrepresent reality. Thus unfortunately we over-

against the deal, that Aixtron's production involves technologies which could be used militarily as well as civilian purposes, is untenable.

Of course the United States—which, in contrast to China, pays more attention to the nominal appreciation of speculative profits than to the real economy—is fearful of losing its military dominance as a superpower with its unipolar demands, but that does not stop it from benefiting monetarily from its geopolitical confrontation with Russia and China at the expense of its allies, on whom it imposes its conditions.

To this end the U.S. Treasury's sanctions czar Adam Szubin visited Berlin, Rome, and Paris last week to argue the importance of maintaining the existing sanctions against Russia. Within German industrial circles it's no secret that, in spite of the sanctions, U.S. industry has increased its trade with Russia, while, for example, the machine tool sector in Baden-Wuerttemberg has recorded a loss of 50% of its exports to Russia—as the former head of German industry's Committee on Eastern European Economic Relations, Klaus Mangold, stressed to the *Schwäbische Zeitung*. If you think about look the fact that the unique opportunity for overcoming that geopolitics—which brought us two world wars in the Twentieth Century and which today, in the era of thermonuclear weapons, can mean the possible extinction of mankind—lies in China's offer of "win-win cooperation" in the development of the New Silk Road. All those who are wearing geopolitical glasses can only project their own geopolitical outlook on others, and cannot imagine that mankind is capable of defining a higher level of reason in which cooperation for mutual benefit is actually possible.

It obviously escaped the intelligence department of the Economics ministry, in its preparations for the trip, that for a good three years, and especially over the last few months, exactly this principle of "win-win cooperation" has progressed by giant steps, leading to a complete realignment of the Asian nations. But that's what comes from taking one's evaluations from such anti-China think tanks as the Mercator Institute for China Studies (MERICS) of the Mercator Foundation, which even recommends selling military equipment to the ASEAN countries, to protect them from China!

Xinhua/Zhang Duo

Chinese Premier Li Keqiang arrives at the airport in Riga, Latvia, Nov. 4, 2016, for an official visit to Latvia and the Fifth Summit of China and Central and Eastern European (CEE) Countries, the "16+1" summit.

China's Offer to the United States

It is not only countries such as Malaysia, Vietnam, Myanmar, Indonesia, and the Philippines that have long since preferred the advantages of economic cooperation with China over the disadvantages of military confrontation with China in the South China Sea. India also figured out long ago that the overtures which the United States and the EU are making toward the "world's most populous democracy," are bringing fewer benefits to India than close collaboration with Russia and China, an alliance which Japan has moved closer to in the recent period.

The 16+1 states in Central and Eastern Europe have likewise finally recognized the opportunities of direct cooperation with China's Silk Road initiative. Thus Latvia, at the Nov. 5 summit in Riga, signed a joint declaration of intent for cooperation with the New Silk Road with Chinese Prime Minister Li Keqiang.

Russian Prime Minister Medvedev has just emphasized, in an interview with Chinese state television (CCTV), that the efforts to fully integrate the Silk Road initiative with the Eurasian Economic Union are moving ahead, and thus offer a completely new perspective for cooperation. It is cooperation through the creation of national markets, and the joint development of high-tech production and new waves of industrialization, in areas which Russia did not have before, but is now compelled to create because of the sanctions.

Everyone who sees the world as it is, and whose perspective has not been distorted by those geopolitical glasses, can see that more and more regions of Eurasia are converging, and thus the vision of a common Eurasian economic space from the Atlantic to the Pacific offers the immediate opportunity for overcoming the war danger through common development. The "win-win cooperation" that China proposes is in no way anti-American, but, since the APEC summit in October of 2014 in Beijing, has been an explicit offer to the United States. The best favor we in Europe can do for the United States is to urge the acceptance of this new paradigm of cooperation.

This article first appeared in German in the weekly Neue Solidarität.

U.S. AND RUSSIA IN SYRIA AND IRAQ

Civilian Casualties and U.S. Hypocrisy

by Carl Osgood

Nov. 7—While the Obama Administration and the American mainstream media have been conducting a wartime black propaganda campaign against Russia, accusing Moscow of committing war crimes in Syria, the reality is that it has been the United States that has been carrying out civilian atrocities—in Iraq and Yemen and Libya—which continue to this day. The attacks on Russia are all part of a larger war drive against Moscow, which also includes the deployment of American and NATO forces to the western borders of Russia in the Baltics, the Black Sea, and Eastern Europe; the deployment of a missile defense system into the region bordering Russia to the south; and the propping up of a virulently anti-Russian neo-Nazi regime in Ukraine, following the 2013 regime change operation in the Maidan Square.

Taken as a whole, the Obama Administration, in the words of Russian Prime Minister Medvedev, has driven U.S.-Russian relations into the pit, to the point that we are on the verge of a World War III of Barack Obama's doing.

It is therefore of special importance to expose the fraud of "Russian atrocities" in Syria, and set the record straight about the United States' own war crimes and crimes against humanity in the Middle East and North Africa region.

Goebbels Propaganda

Nearly every day, the Western news media, along with its Middle East fellow travelers such as Al Jazeera, pump out lurid stories claiming that Russian jets are indiscriminately bombing civilians in Syria, especially in Aleppo, and that the government of Bashar al Assad is waging war on its own people. Human rights organizations regularly accuse the Syrian government and the

Russian military of bombing schools and hospitals on an almost daily basis. U.S. Secretary of State John Kerry and other diplomats have called for war crimes investigations of Russian military actions in Syria, particularly focussed on Aleppo. At the same time, there is almost no accounting of the civilian casualties caused by anti-government groups, other than the Islamic State, and by U.S. and U.S.-led coalition military actions in both Syria and Iraq, particularly since the Russian military intervention began in Syria on Sept. 30, 2015.

Civilian Casualties in Syria

The Syrian Observatory for Human Rights calculated on Sept. 30, 2016 that a grand total of 9,364 people had been killed during the first year of the Russian mil-

Combat vehicle participates in NATO field training exercise Silver Arrow in Latvia, Oct. 2016.

itary intervention in Syria. Of the 9,364, 2,746 had been members of the Islamic State, while 2,814 had been from various Islamist and other anti-government groups. The remaining 3,804 were civilians.

The Syrian Observatory, run by Rami Abdulrahman out of his apartment in Coventry, England, is no disinterested observer of the Syrian war, but rather is a British-sponsored propaganda outlet that is supporting regime change in Damascus and, therefore, has every reason to exaggerate the number of civilian casualties in Syria resulting from the war. The Syrian Observatory, in fact, has long been the "go to" source for the Western media for body count numbers, especially of deaths inflicted by government forces and their Russian allies, numbers which they never make any effort to verify. Yet, 3,804 civilian deaths over a one-year period in an intense urban conflict is the most that the Observatory could come up with.

While every civilian death in war is a tragedy, the number of 3,804, if true, pales in comparison with the mayhem inflicted on Iraq, during and after the U.S. invasion of March 2003. While the U.S. military, today, frequently claims that it takes every report of civilian deaths inflicted by U.S. munitions very seriously, the Rumsfeld Pentagon famously refused to keep track of the numbers of civilians that were dying daily, as a result of the U.S. military intervention, a factor which no doubt has increased the difficulty in accounting for the suffering of civilians in Iraq. Numerous studies have been done over the years, and while the findings of these studies often conflict with each other, it is obvious that U.S. military actions in Iraq have been far deadlier than what the Russians have been accused of in Syria.

A research team from the Bloomberg School of Public Health at Johns Hopkins University, published in *The Lancet* on Oct. 28, 2004, estimated that 100,000 civilians had died from the direct and indirect consequences of the U.S. war and occupation. Among the findings was that violence had replaced heart attacks, strokes, and chronic disease as the leading cause of death in Iraq, compared to before the U.S. invasion. In 2006, the same team of researchers upped its estimate

UNHCR/Ivor Prickett

As Mosul assault begins, internally displaced persons flee to Debaga camp in Northern Iraq.

to a staggering 600,000 deaths, based on an even much larger sampling of households than was used for the 2004 survey.

In 2008, the World Health Organization concluded that there had been 151,000 deaths, which only added to the fierce controversy over the impacts of the U.S. invasion and occupation. Regardless of which study one accepts, however, the impact of the U.S. war on Iraq has been much greater than the 3,800 civilians that the Syrian Observatory counted killed in the first year of the Russian military intervention in Syria. Yet there have been no calls for war crimes investigations of the United States from agencies of the United Nations or from international human rights groups.

Virginia State Senator Richard Black, a Vietnam veteran and a former officer in the Army Judge Advocate General Corps, said in a Nov. 4 interview with LPAC TV, that the Syrian Observatory figure of 3,800 civilians deaths is probably accurate, because it's so *astonishingly low*. The U.S. invasion of Iraq, on the other hand, produced much higher casualties because it was based on "shock and awe." The term "shock and awe," Black pointed out, actually has a military meaning:

> What you do is attack every agency that can assist people, every place that they can look to for help. You bomb bridges. You bomb roads. You bomb electrical power stations. You "accidently" bomb hospitals, I don't think we inten-

tionally bombed hospitals but we bombed a few hospitals. We bombed government offices, police offices, any place that a person in desperation would go … There was no place to call, no means of communication, all the radio stations, TV stations, were bombed out. So, we did this shock and awe campaign.

In contrast to the U.S. campaign in Iraq, "I think what you see in the Syrian Russian campaign is a considerable degree of caution about killing civilians," Black said, citing his own

UNHCR/Ivor Prickett

An Iraqi family displaced by fighting in the village of Shora flees towards an Iraqi army checkpoint.

experience in Vietnam with fighting an enemy that fights among the population. "When you're in battle and the enemy chooses to fight in an occupied area, there will be civilians killed. It's going to happen in Mosul," in Iraq, where the United States is now leading a campaign against ISIS, "and it will happen to a much greater extent than what is happening now in Aleppo," Black said.

U.S. War Crimes in Iraq and Yemen

The Russians, in fact, are watching the U.S. military campaign in Mosul very closely. On Nov. 3, Lt. Gen. Sergei Rudskoi, the chief of the Main Operational Directorate of the Russian General Staff, presented, in a briefing at the Defense Ministry, two sets of before-and-after satellite images of residential areas near Mosul that had been hit by U.S. air strikes. "The United States continues to make strikes on residential quarters both in Mosul and in other inhabited areas of the Nineveh province of Iraq," he said.

Rudskoi, in an earlier briefing on Oct. 25, reported that the Russian Defense Ministry knew "about numerous facts of the U.S.-led coalition's air strikes against living quarters, schools, and other civil infrastructure buildings both in Mosul and in other settlements in Iraq's Nineveh governorate." Rudskoi continued, "In the past three days alone, more than 60 civilians, in-

cluding children, fell victim of these air strikes. More than 200 people have been wounded."

Russian foreign ministry spokeswoman Maria Zakharova issued a particularly sharp criticism of the U.S.-led campaign in a statement posted on her Facebook page on Nov. 6:

> The operation is being conducted in conditions of absolute information blockade as the coalition provides no reliable information about what is going on there. It is absolutely not clear whether the coalition forces are advancing or retreating, how efficient their tactic is, what are their losses, how many sorties were flown, and by whom.

According to Zakharova, civilians are dying from the actions of both militants and the coalition forces confronting them, making a "medieval massacre" of the anti-terrorist operation. The situation is worsened by the lack of systemic approach to evacuation of civilians. "It has turned out that no comprehensive plan for the evacuation of civilians has been elaborated. Nothing like humanitarian corridors has been provided," she stressed.

But it isn't just the Russians who are making these accusations. Jürgen Todenhöfer—the German journalist who, with his son, famously spent several weeks inside ISIS-occupied Syria in 2014-2015—estimated, in an angry post on his Facebook page on Oct. 25, that 15,000 civilians have already died in Mosul because of U.S. bombing, which has been going on there for more than two years, and yet, unlike in Aleppo, the world is silent while tens of thousands more civilians will likely die. U.S. bombing has already destroyed electricity, gas and water supplies, hospitals, and universities. In Todenhöfer's estimate, 50,000 civilians have been killed by U.S. bombing in Iraq (including Mosul) since 2014, and the cities that have previously been "freed" from ISIS, such as Ramadi and Tikrit, haven't been freed, so much as destroyed, with nothing for their former residents to return to.

UNHCR/Yahya Arhab

In Yemen, internally displaced children in Darwin camp, Amran province, after their family fled their home in Saada province.

In Yemen, where the United States is backing a Saudi-led bombing campaign on behalf of an exiled government, UN relief officials and the World Food Program (WFP) reported last week that 7.1 million Yemenis are threatened with starvation. UN aid chief Stephen O'Brien stated that, "Yemen is one step away from famine," according to a report by *Vice News*. Eighty percent of Yemen is currently in need of humanitarian assistance, and 19 of the country's 22 governates have reached crisis levels of food insecurity, according to the WFP. Due to the closure of the airport in the capital city of Sana'a; Saudi-led coalition border blockades; and repeated bombings of farms, wells, and agriculture, food supplies have dwindled.

"Malnourished children are exceeding the capacity of our centers," George Khoury, the director of the UN's Office for the Coordination of Humanitarian Affairs in Yemen, told *Vice News*. "While the conduct of hostility is one factor for deaths and killing, the major factor is not war in Yemen. People are dying silently every day because of malnutrition."

U.S. Congressman Ted Lieu, Democrat from California, has warned repeatedly that the U.S. participation in the Saudi campaign means that America is participating in war crimes in Yemen—including the numerous episodes of bombings of civilian sites—by providing key military support to the Saudis. In a Nov. 2 letter to Secretary of State John Kerry and Secretary

of Defense Ashton Carter, Lieu wrote:

By now, the United States has knowledge that in the past 18 months, coalition jets have struck civilian targets multiple times. Amnesty International and Human Rights Watch have already documented at least 70 unlawful air strikes by the coalition on civilian targets, such as children at school, a wedding party, a civilian market, and multiple hospitals.

Lieu warned, therefore, that,

U.S. personnel are now at legal risk of being investigated and potentially prosecuted for committing war crimes. Under international law, a person can be found guilty of aiding and abetting war crimes.

Russia Responds to U.S. Hypocrisy

In contrast, in Aleppo the Russians have refrained from air strikes against opposition-held parts of the city for the past 20 days—despite a terrorist offensive intended to try to break the government siege of those parts of the city—and have opened up humanitarian corridors for civilians to leave, and even for militants to either quit the insurgency or get safe passage to opposition-held Idlib province. The insurgents, who are dominated by the Jabhat Fateh al Sham, the group formerly known as the Al Qaeda-affiliated Jabhat al Nusra, and who are directed from Turkey and Saudi Arabia, have not only refused to leave, but have actively worked to prevent civilians from leaving, by directing sniper and mortar fire on the corridors.

Nonetheless, the U.S. State Department is completely unsatisfied with what the Russians have done. The "humanitarian pause [in the bombing of Aleppo] was designed for what?" asked State Department spokesman John Kirby on Nov. 4. He continued:

> To allow people to leave, but it was also to allow aid to get in. And how much aid has gotten in? None. And so we're seeing reports now of citizens of Aleppo tying ropes around their abdomens to try to get around the abdominal pain that they're feeling from starvation. They're going to contaminated water sources for drinking water, because there isn't any. What little hospitals there are in Aleppo are now being forced underground into basements, and the medical personnel that are staffing them, we're seeing reports now, of them having to use non-sanitized equipment to try to tend wounds and to try to make people feel better … So whether the pause is in effect or not, you'd have to talk to the Russians. But the Syrian people, particularly the citizens of Aleppo, certainly aren't feeling any benefits from it.

In an angry reply to these U.S. allegations the next day, Russian Defense Ministry spokesman Maj. Gen. Igor Konashenkov began by asking, What has the State Department done for the people of Aleppo? He continued:

> During this period of time, the United States has not even met the obligations it assumed under the agreements between Russia and the United States. Russia has never received either maps, or positions, or any other information about any terrorist organization in Syria: from the Islamic State to Al Nusra.

IRIN/Tom Westcott

Syrians remaining in Aleppo are too poor to leave, living in the carcasses of apartment blocks. In recent months, Russian forces delivered over 100 tons of food and medications.

Statements such as Kirby's, he said,

> once again demonstrate how differently the State Department and we understand "the use" of humanitarian pauses … Over the past months only, we have delivered more than 100 tonnes of most important aid—foods, medications, and essentials. This was delivered to all citizens of Aleppo, not limited to its western or eastern part. Meanwhile, the State Department has not delivered a mite to Syrians it is allegedly so much caring for.

In fact, Russian helicopters have been shot at, with at least two, perhaps more, shot down while on missions to deliver humanitarian aid, while a number of Russian military personnel have been killed. Last week, three Russian soldiers were wounded by mortar fire at one of the humanitarian corridor checkpoints in Aleppo. The Russians are in Syria, taking these risks to reduce civilian casualties, as the full partner of the recognized Syrian government in Damascus. The United States, on the other hand, as in the case of Iraq in 2003, has been the invader far more than it has been an invited partner. The result of U.S. military actions has been a spiral of violence and suffering imposed on civilian populations across the entire region from Libya to Afghanistan, the consequence of a criminal policy.

Modern Egypt and the United States: What They Never Told You

by Dennis Speed

Nov. 9—In a presentation given to the October 29 Schiller Institute conference, "In the Footsteps of Alexander Hamilton: A New, Just America and a World Governed by Reason," Ambassador Ahmed Farouk, Consul General of Egypt in New York, advanced an important, central conception in his speech on "The History, Ideology, and Development of Radical Movements in the Middle East." Ambassador Farouk described the history of conflict in northern Africa, Southwest Asia, and other Islamic faith based territories as divided between "the reformers" and "the awakeners." The former advocate modern civil society and believe in the gradual improvement of society by means of technological and scientific progress, in harmony with, but not dominated by a particular theological worldview. The latter believe that society can only be organized as a theocratic state, and that that state is perpetually at war with any other body that is not of that theocratic persuasion. Modernity, advancement, is their sworn enemy.

By identifying this key concept, Ambassador Farouk properly placed the "Middle Eastern conflict," as well as the "Clash of Civilizations" conflict, outside of Islam as such. In fact, his idea is fully congruent with one that which *Executive Intelligence Review* founder Lyndon LaRouche formulated in a ground breaking book length essay in 1978, "The Secrets Known Only to the Inner Elites"—the battle throughout the 2,500 years of Western Civilization between the Platonists and the Aristotelians. It is sometimes called the battle between the "city-builders" and the "empire-builders." It is in fact the age old battle

Muhammad Ali, 1769-1849, Khedive of Egypt

between those on the side of human creativity, progress, discovery, and invention, and the "back to the land," "back to the cave," "back to nature" oligarchies of history.

Today it is exemplified in the battle between the pro-nuclear/thermonuclear energy, population-growth forces, and the anti-nuclear/thermonuclear population-reduction forces. Egypt's recent history, that is, its past 250 years, has embodied this battle.

Modern Egypt

Subjugated by the Ottoman Empire in 1517, Egypt saw a new day with the rise to power of the great Mohammad Ali (1769-1849). A self proclaimed leader of Egypt, who rose to power without the consent of the Ottoman caliphate, Ali was also not stopped by British and French imperialism from modernizing Egypt. Improvements in agriculture; irrigation and water management; industry; and the military marked his rule, which extended from 1805 until 1848. In Ambassador Farouk's speech, he referenced Ali's modernization program, including his sending of students to Europe for engineering, medical, and veterinary studies. Mohammad Ali's grandson, Ismail Pasha, would later oversee the creation of the Suez Canal, built by Egypt with French engineers from 1859 to 1869.

It is noteworthy that the recent "doubling expansion" of the Suez Canal, which has redrawn the world map for global commerce and trade, was successfully completed in one year, an engineering feat that has amazed and inspired the world. This is another example of the "city builder" orientation of the present Egyptian government.

In introducing Ambassador Farouk, Dennis Speed, Schiller Institute Northeast representative, documented the recruitment by Ismail Pasha, Khedive of Egypt and the builder of the Suez Canal, of 50 American former Union and Confederate military officers. The Khedive had approached Thaddeus Mott, a West Point graduate. He was serving in the Ottoman army after the Civil War was over; he was the son of a prominent physician. He had obtained permission from Grant's Army Chief of Staff Gen. William Tecumseh Sherman, to recruit a team to go to Egypt. These veterans from both sides of the recently concluded American war of 1861 65, joined forces as engineers, surveyors, educators, explorers, and military advisers, for a nine year "tour of duty," from 1869 until 1878.

Ambassador Ahmed Farouk, Consul General of Egypt in New York.

President Ulysses Grant—whose Administration had authorized the delegation—visited Egypt and that American delegation in the final year of the official American presence there. The important point is that the Americans *built things*. They did a lot of surveying, they tamed many rivers, they mapped parts of the Nile River tributary system, they built many roads. And most important, the educational system, particularly for the nation's military, was largely reorganized, using the West Point model.

So when you talk about the Egyptian military today and you hear criticisms of a certain type, you have to realize that often the critics don't even recognize that the national identity and the sense of patriotism that you see being expressed there, used to be *here*. It was an export; it was the kind of thing that when America was good, it used to export: a sense of mission, a sense of purpose, a sense of national identity, and a sense that the uplifting of a people, the self development of a people, is the most important commodity that one can export, rather than talking merely about something abstract and empty, like

"democracy." It's a nice term, but as the poet Friedrich Schiller once said, "if you give a man food, clothing, and shelter, dignity will come of itself."

The Muslim Brotherhood

Ambassador Farouk spent much of his talk discussing the Muslim Brotherhood, an organization founded in Egypt in 1929. His reference prompted a review of *EIR*'s extensive archive on the topic, a file that began in the mid 1970s. The following are observations, entirely independent of the ambassador's presentation, intended to provide the reader with a broader acquaintance with the topic. The British Intelligence origins of that organization is key. That background is in part supplied here.

The Muslim Brotherhood is thought of as the immediate ancestor of the radical Islamic organizations that have spread over the globe in the last 60 years, and particularly after its suppression in Egypt in 1954. Hassan al Banna, born in 1906, was the founder of the Muslim Brotherhood.

The British East India Company, nearly from its inception in 1763, supported those factions in Islam that were considered to best cohere with the designs of the

Dredgers and elevators at work on the construction of the Suez Canal.

Empire and its demand that colonized or soon to be colonized populations should have little or no access to anything resembling economic independence. The Company wanted to find the most backward elements willing to impose upon themselves the cultural self stagnation that supported the looting policies of British monetarism. This tactic was not original with Britain. The ancient monetary center of Babylon—"the Whore of Babylon"—and Mesopotamia more generally, had been noted for its practice of "god building"—the export of cult beliefs to subjugated territories in order to install a belief system that justified the "tribute to the gods" (gold, currency, cattle, land) that would be collected by the imperial center.

During the 1820s, "god building" became a systematized project of British Intelligence, known as "the Oxford Movement." As Robert Dreyfuss explained,

> The chief sponsors of the British cult building project during this period were the British royal family itself and many of its leading prime ministers and aides, such as Benjamin Disraeli, Lord Palmerston, Lord Shaftesbury, and Edward Bulwer Lytton.... Bulwer Lytton, who served as the head of Britain's Colonial Office and India Office for years and was then succeeded by his son, was a practicing member of the ancient cult of Isis and Osiris ... This paragon of the "empire builder" is the grandfather of the pre Raphaelite Brotherhood of John Ruskin, and many other organizations ...[1]

The actual founders and Islamic precursors of the Muslim Brotherhood in the 1920s were often themselves victims of the "Orientalists" of the British Crown's Oxford and Cambridge universities. British intelligence agent Jamaleddin al Afghani, active from 1857 until 1897, was the immediate intellectual ancestor of the Muslim Brotherhood. He synthesized Sufism, the Baha'i

Hasan al-Banna, 1906-1949, was a school teacher and imam, and is best known as the founder of the Muslim Brotherhood.

faith, freemasonry, and Islam as a syncretic cover for his intelligence assignments, given to him by E.G. Browne, head of Cambridge University's Oriental Languages Department.

One of Browne's proteges was Harry St. John Philby, "Philby of Arabia," also known as Sheikh Abdullah, an adviser to the Wahhabist Ibn Saud from 1917—the same Ibn Saud who later became head of the family enterprise known as Saudi Arabia. So, while it is true that in 1927, Hasan al Banna co founded the Young Men's Muslim Association, which in 1929 became the Society of Muslim Brothers—today's Muslim Brotherhood—the true founders of the Muslim Brotherhood were in reality British intelligence's St. John Philby, Sir John Glubb Pasha, T.E. Lawrence, and the "god-builders" of the 1820s Oxford Movement.

This background is essential to situate the causal principle behind the otherwise bewildering divisions and subdivisions that appear to exist, for example, in the Syrian conflict. While there are many sectarian divisions within Islam, the phenomenon called "radical Islam" is a British intelligence spawned artificial phenomenon introduced into Islam by "Londonistan," the true center of world terrorism, and its "Arab Bureau," as expressed in the British Saudi Al Yamamah deal, or in the personage of Saudi Prince Bandar bin Sultan, who figures as a central player in the events of September 11, 2001.

When U.S. Presidents Were Not British Puppets

American policy toward Egypt has not always been a moral disaster. Sixty years ago, in 1956, President Dwight D. Eisenhower risked his re election when he defended Egypt's national sovereignty in the Suez Canal crisis, at the point that the British and French governments, in response to President Gamal Abdel Nasser's July nationalization of the canal, worked in tandem with the Israeli military and attempted to wrest the canal from Egypt.

Eisenhower recognized the actions of the Egyptian government to be sovereign and legal. When it became

---

1. Robert Dreyfuss, *Hostage to Khomeini* (1981), p. 114.

UK Imperial War Museums

Smoke rises from oil tanks beside the Suez Canal that were hit during the initial Anglo-French assault on Port Said, November 5, 1956.

clear that both France and Britain intended military action against Egypt, Eisenhower "wondered if the hand of Churchill might not be behind this—inasmuch as this action is in the mid Victorian style." Eisenhower had the United States introduce a resolution into the United Nations on November 1, 1956—the day after London began bombing Egypt—that condemned the Israeli occupation of Gaza and the West Bank on the border with Jordan. Eisenhower actively considered deploying the American military capability to assist Egypt if necessary, and supported United Nations sanctions against Israel.

Contrast the actions of a President Eisenhower, acting in the true interests of the United States, to the spectacle of Barack Obama's *de facto* support of "radical Islam"—that is, British intelligence's "Islamic fundamentalism card," the same forces that were incited by Obama supporter and Carter Administration national security advisor Zbigniew Brzezinski in 1979, on the border of Pakistan and Afghanistan, to conduct a jihad against the Soviet Union. Look at the effect of that Obama support of "radical Islam" in Libya and Syria, as well as the spin off effects in places like Chad, Niger, and northern Nigeria. Look at the near disastrous effect of the Obama Administration's *de facto* earlier support for the Muslim Brotherhood in Egypt. Contrast Egypt then, in 2012 2013, to Egypt now.

Despite recent pressures placed on Egypt through the IMF—as well as the temporary setback to Egypt's expectations as the trade and commercial benefits from the doubling of the Suez Canal are yet to be realized—what is important is that Egypt has stood for the tradition of the city builder, of the future a future without war, and without fanaticism. The "General Welfare" of the people of Egypt, not short-term relief in acquiescence to debt slavery, was the narrow path chosen.

Immortality of Purpose: the True Divine Spark

What, then, might represent—in addition to the policy of the World Land Bridge pioneered by Lyndon and Helga LaRouche worldwide since 1989—a means for people in Egypt and throughout Southwest Asia to "out-flank" the paralysis of the cultural backwardness upon which the ideology of radicalism feeds?

In a 1982 document entitled, "A Doctrine of Constitutional Law for the Iranian Renaissance from the Dark Age of Neo Asharite Irrationalism," Lyndon LaRouche spoke about the identity of the truly human individual:

As we trace the progressive development of the divine potential within the individual, over the course of a normal childhood, adolescence, and adulthood, we define three general levels of correlated moral intellectual maturation, corresponding to the three canticles of Dante's *Commedia*: "Inferno," "Purgatory," and "Paradise." These are categories elaborated in St. Augustine's writings, and are the "bronze," "silver," and "golden" souls of Socrates' Phoenician myths in Plato's *Republic*.

The adult level of moral development, the "Paradise" of the *Commedia*, is the level of development in which the individual locates his or her self interest in the non-ephemeral consequences of his or her developed judgement for practice. The development of the individual capacities and scope for efficient practice of such an individual person becomes, for such a person, the necessary (ephemeral, mortal) instrumentality, the means by which the non ephemeral, true self interest is realized: the "philosopher king" of Plato's dialogue is an example of a fully developed intellect of such moral characteristic.

In a different section of the same document—in a section entitled, "The Heritage of Al Farabi"—a discussion of the principles of Classical musical composition specifically discussing the great Islamic scholar Al Farabi (870 950 AD) and his Grand Book of Music (*Kitab al Musiqui al Kabila*)—LaRouche expresses the ecumenical character of the "musical principle" that has characterized his Manhattan Project of the past twenty-four months:

The form of well tempered polyphony associated with Zarlino, Bach, Mozart, and Beethoven, was developed in Europe through employing the design of the well tempered system specified by al Farabi to fulfill the specifications for music defined by St. Augustine. Yet al Farabi correctly insists that his octave scale ordered by fifths is very ancient at the time al Farabi wrote. In fact, the principles of well tempered two voice polyphony were already established before Plato among the Greeks, and existed in China centuries before the Han dynasty …

Kepler's proof that the Solar system has been composed according to the same principles known for music to al Farabi does more than suggest that the well tempered octave scale is the only mode for human music. Well tempered polyphony is the only possible form of music: assuming one understands the relationship of modal forms of composition to the well tempered system.

There is a universal cultural expression, through human music, of the identity of the human race. In the same way, "the book of nature," especially Galactic space, and the potential discoveries embedded therein, can be read by all nations, and applied by all nations, whose citizens are made capable of imparting and receiving new scientific principles of human practice.

Economics derives from these two primary sciences of creativity, and is only properly thought of as the science of the reproduction of the human species at higher and higher levels of what LaRouche has called poten-tial relative population density. More people, at a higher living standard, with a greater surplus per cycle of production and per square unit of area, can be maintained on the surface of the planet. There is no population crisis. The greater the density of population, and the greater the potential of that economy to increase that population density relative to an earlier phase of society's development, the more successful an economy is. The universal comprehension and propagation of the principle of potential relative population density would render war impotent and obsolete, and would cause terrorism and fanaticism to wither away.

The idea of Constitutional law that LaRouche presents here is the same as that which he has sought to revive in recent weeks with his restatement of the principles embodied in Alexander Hamilton's seminal works on economics: his Treasury reports of 1790 on manufactures, public credit, the national bank, the mint, and the constitutionality of the bank.

The LaRouche Four Laws are not merely "economic principles," but a statement of the immortal purpose of government, as stated in the Preamble to the Constitution of the United States and its General Welfare clause, "to secure the blessings of Liberty to ourselves and our posterity." In a republic, the citizen must have the right to be treated as an adult, and has, in turn, the duty to act as an adult. That means that the principles of self government, which begin with an apprehension of truth by means of scientific experiment, are knowable and reproducible—not the products of a religious belief, or mystical, "ecstatic" experience.

An immortal principle need not be stated in solely religious terms. The compositions of Mozart, Beethoven, and Brahms, and the work of true scientist musicians such as Albert Einstein, demonstrate this. It must necessarily be so, otherwise scientific principles could not be universal. Alexander Hamilton established a science of republican economic self government through his Reports.

If the LaRouche Four Laws are read among the Egyptian population with the same vigor and intensity that we have seen in the demonstrations of recent years, it would be possible to restart the collaboration that the Khedive of Egypt and President Grant enjoyed 150 years ago. Further dialogues, such as that of October 29, and involving other nations as well, will substantially improve the prospects for such a happy, and revolutionary, occurrence.

www.ingramcontent.com/pod-product-compliance
Lightning Source LLC
Chambersburg PA
CBHW051952280526
45789CB00009B/3264